Original title:
Rooted Reflections

Copyright © 2025 Creative Arts Management OÜ
All rights reserved.

Author: Alec Davenport
ISBN HARDBACK: 978-1-80567-244-9
ISBN PAPERBACK: 978-1-80567-543-3

Pathways of the Past

In the garden of my youth, I played,
Mud pies and mischief, unafraid.
The trees whispered secrets, oh so tall,
I'd climb them high, then promptly fall.

A bicycle ride, a scrape on the knee,
Every corner a new mystery.
Grass stains on pants, a badge of pride,
Memories bloom, like daisies wide.

Whispers of the Underground

In tunnels so cozy, the gossip is grand,
While moles plot a heist for some soft, juicy land.
They chuckle 'bout sunlight and taste of the rain,
While badgers in sunglasses discuss their next gain.

A party of mushrooms throws shadows at night,
With fireflies buzzing, they bring out the light.
"There's magic in dirt," says a wise old tree,
"Let's toast to all roots, and the giggles they see!"

Echoes Beneath the Surface

Beneath the green grass, a party unfolds,
With worms wearing tuxes, exchanging some gold.
They dance in the dirt, with mud on their face,
Claiming they're royalty in their own spacious place.

A rock band of crickets starts strumming a tune,
The ants stomp along, making dust clouds like moons.
The roots wiggle and giggle in this festive affair,
As whispers of laughter float high in the air.

Deeply Anchored Dreams

In gardens of night, dreams take a stroll,
With flowers that giggle and dance on a pole.
They whisper of secrets, of where they should roam,
While snails on high horses say, 'This is our home!'

When daisies decide to throw a big bash,
They invite sleeping bees, but watch for the splash.
The sun, dressed in shades, rolls up with a grin,
Saying, 'Let's plant stories where laughter begins!'

The Bounty Beneath

Deep under the soil, a treasure is found,
With potatoes who party, and onions that clown.
A turnip recites the best jokes of the land,
While carrots play checkers, with celery planned.

They bury their treasures, in laughter they bask,
In the bounty of burrows, they've no need to ask.
For veggies who giggle and dance to the tune,
Find joy in their digging, beneath the full moon.

Reflection in the Roots

Reflections in puddles can cause quite a fuss,
Especially when frogs think they're one of us.
Roots whisper secrets to trees overhead,
While squirrels discuss breakfast, a little misled.

The mirror of ground tells of who's in the game,
A dandelion dreaming of fortune and fame.
Who knew such ambitions could come from the dirt?
Yet they flower in laughter, with plans that divert!

Intersections of Legacy

Where paths intersect, stories collide,
Old roots graze the surface, with nowhere to hide.
A legacy's tangled—like yarn in a cat,
Each twist a strange tale, or a joke with a spat.

Uncle Henry once swore he could fly on a kite,
But ended up stuck in a tree for a night.
So spread the tales freely, let laughter unfurl,
At each intersection, watch nonsense whirl!

Gardens of the Mind

In a garden of thoughts, weeds do sprout,
The flowers of ideas stomp about.
Sunshine bursts laughter, rain brings a sigh,
Even daisies can giggle and try to fly.

A cactus with jokes, oh so prickly and bright,
Tells puns that can pierce you, such a funny sight.
The daisies are dancing, while roses just pout,
In gardens of nonsense, with laughs all about.

In the Grit of Growth

With dirt on my hands and state of bliss,
I dug up weeds; oh, what a twist!
Planted a seed thinking I'm a pro,
But all I got was a spicy tomato show.

In the sun, I swear there's a dance,
As flowers sway, taking their chance.
Dear carrots, sprouting, oh what a sight,
Wishing me luck while munching on light.

Connections to the Earth

I tried to plant a tree last spring,
But ended up with a stubborn thing.
It sat there sulking, rooted so deep,
I think it's plotting while I sleep.

Grumpy shrubs with their leafy frowns,
Plotting rebellion in garden towns.
Yet here I stand with my watering can,
Hoping one day they'll understand my plan.

Nature's Chronicle

The flowers gossip in the breeze,
"Oh look, it's another couple of bees!"
With bumblebees buzzing, a fluffy parade,
Nature's tales are never delayed.

Rabbits hop with a skip and a grin,
Watching the world, they wriggle in.
Ants marching home with their crumbs of bread,
Planning a feast, in their tiny heads.

Silent Growth

In a world of stillness, whispers arise,
With sprouts sharing tales of their dream-tinged skies.
A snail sends a postcard, 'Wish you were here!'
While seedlings share laughter, sipping on cheer.

In corners of quiet, secrets do bloom,
As shadows tell stories of what's in the room.
The chatter of petals fills soft with delight,
While the sun whispers, 'Grow, and dance in the light!'

Continuity in the Canopy

In the forest, I took a stroll,
Tripping over a squirrel's bowl.
He rolled his eyes, a snack in hand,
And scolded me for not being planned.

With branches dancing in the breeze,
I asked a tree for tips, if you please!
It said, 'Just bend, don't break, be wise,'
As I pondered low-hanging fruit in disguise.

The leaves above laughed at my plight,
A bird chimed in, 'That's not quite right!'
'You're here to learn and stay awhile,'
That funny tree, it made me smile.

Now I know when life gets quirky,
Embrace the odd, it's far less murky.
In every twist, let laughter soar,
For even roots have room to explore.

Branches of Memory

In the attic, a hat from the past,
It fits like a charm, though it's way too vast.
Old photos are laughing, what a silly sight,
Remembering times when we danced through the night.

Grandma's old broomstick, she claimed it could fly,
But we saw her trip, oh my, did she cry!
The stories we tell, with a wink and a grin,
Are branches of laughter, where joy starts to spin.

Seasons of the Soul

Springtime is sneezing, the flowers are bright,
Pollen's invading! Oh, what a plight!
Summer's here laughing, with ice cream galore,
But bees are plotting, oh, they're such a bore.

Autumn leaves dive, like they're in a race,
While winter shivers with a frozen face.
Each season a giggle, each moment a jest,
Life's wacky parade, oh, we're truly blessed.

Fertile Ground of Dreams

In the garden of wishes, a gnome sits and grins,
He whispers to daisies, where magic begins.
The carrots are chatting, the radishes cheer,
While tomatoes debate who's the freshest here!

The soil's a comedian, it cracks when it dries,
Each sprout is a punchline, what a surprise!
Dreams grow like weeds, oh, the fun that we seek,
With laughter as water, we're never too weak.

Traces of Forgotten Paths

Once we wandered, with a map drawn in crayon,
Lost in the woods, oh the tales we ran on!
A squirrel named Gary stole our last snack,
Now he's a legend, we want our cheese back!

Footprints of memories, they wander and play,
With shadows of laughter that dance in the fray.
Each turn we abused, led to giggles and cheer,
For the paths that we stroll, are the best souvenirs.

Rewinds of Resilience

In the garden of mishaps, we dance with glee,
Falling flat on our faces, oh what a spree!
With each stumble and trip, we learn to bounce,
Life's a circus, we laugh, and just pounce.

Once tripped over roots that twisted with glee,
A slide down the hill, what a sight to see!
Yet every old bruise tells a tale of cheer,
In the rewinds of life, we gather near.

With every setback that makes us feel blue,
We briefly hit pause, then we start anew.
So here's to the laughter, the fumbles we share,
In the rewinds of resilience, there's love everywhere.

So spill your own soup, let it fly through the air,
Join in the laughter, life's far too rare.
We navigate hiccups, like pro clowns we roll,
In the circus of life, it fills up the soul.

Ancestral Footprints

Upon the old trails, my family did roam,
With tales of their quirks, they brought laughter home.
From tripping on roots, to falling in streams,
They left me with legends, and wild, wacky dreams.

Ancestors of mine, with their antics galore,
With faces like clowns and a flair for folklore,
They passed on the jokes, the wisdom and fun,
In their goofy pursuits, we all came undone.

Their paths paved with giggles, oh what a delight,
They danced through the shadows, they danced through the light.
Stomped in puddles, told tales that were bold,
Every footprint was laughter, a treasure to hold.

So here's to the mischief, the humor they spread,
Their paths map out joy, that's how laughter's bred.
With each step I take, I chuckle with glee,
For my ancestral footprint keeps tickling me.

Entwined Histories

In tangled threads of stories, our giggles unfurl,
Like a family tree that's a top-notch whirl.
With branches of blunders that twist and entwine,
Our heritage sparkles like vintage red wine.

Each ancestor's tale a hilarious twist,
From questionable dances to rhymes that we missed.
We weave through our memories, both silly and grand,
As we chuckle together, united we stand.

The missteps and fumbles, they bind us the most,
Creating a mixture of laughter and boast.
From eaten-up homework to wild family nights,
The humor in chaos gives life such delights.

So grab a popcorn kernel, let's spin the old yarn,
In the quilt of our lives, each patch is a charm.
Entwined through our laughter, a tapestry strong,
We cherish these moments, where we all belong.

Layers of Experience

Life's layers are funny, like cake gone awry,
With frosting and sprinkles that dance to the sky.
Each slice tells a story, both messy and sweet,
From slipping on icing to cinnamon feet.

We pile up the lessons, each one is a treat,
With flavors of failure, oh life's so replete!
From spicy mischief to chocolate delight,
In the kitchen of chaos, we stir through the night.

With anecdotes stacked like a tower we build,
Each layer a laugh, with pure joy, we're filled.
So pass me a fork, and let's dig right in,
In the layers of fun, that's where we begin.

So here's to the moments, the giggles, the cheer,
In layers of experience, we find we are here.
Life's a banquet of laughter, both savory and bright,
We feast on the joy, oh what a delight!

Grounding the Spirit

In a garden, I found a worm,
Wiggling along, all full of charm.
Said, "You think you've got it rough?"
"I can dig it! It's not that tough!"

A cactus laughed, its needles laid bare,
"Fear not, my friend, I'm prickly with flair!"
"While you dig deep, I stand so tall,"
"Just try, little worm, to take a fall!"

With roots that stretch and minds that twist,
We ponder life and laugh at the list.
"What's the point?" the plant-people sigh,
"Wait, is it lunch? Pass that pizza by!"

So here we rest with our funny dreams,
Amongst the dirt, where laughter gleams.
With quirky roots and silly airs,
Grounding the spirit has its own flares!

Nature's Mirror

The pond reflects a froggy pose,
"I might be warty, but check my nose!"
Said lily pads with a mock-faint,
"Oh darling, you could be a saint!"

A squirrel above snickered with glee,
"Mirror, mirror, who's the best tree?"
With chattering branches and leaves so bright,
"I'm the one who dances in the light!"

The flowers giggled, swaying their heads,
"We're the stars! Enough with your spreads!"
"How do you bloom? Show us your tricks!"
"Just wiggle and giggle, it's in the mix!"

Laughter echoed through nature's stage,
Each reflection a moment to engage.
With joyous blooms and critters bold,
Like mirrors, we share the laughter untold!

Whispers Beneath the Surface

Beneath the ground, the whispers tease,
"Did you hear what that plant said with ease?"
"I'm trying my best to grow quite tall,"
"But my neighbor here keeps blocking my call!"

The roots conspired, a tangled mess,
"Let's plant a joke, it's anyone's guess!"
"Why did the sunflower cross the way?"
"To take a selfie in the light of day!"

The ants marched by, all straight and neat,
"We're the workers, can't be beat!"
With tiny helmets and briefcase dreams,
"Our life's a blast of laugh-out-loud themes!"

From below the surface, laughter does rise,
Nature narrates the funniest ties.
When roots get feisty, and spirits collide,
Whispers bring joy, our secret aside!

Tides of Time

The waves rolled in with a cheeky grin,
"Wave after wave, let the fun begin!"
The sandcastles giggled, losing their crown,
"We're the kings, let's not drown!"

Seagulls squawked their melodious tunes,
"Is it snack time? Let's swoon like loons!"
With fish jumping, a sight so divine,
"Who's got the catch? Looks like dinner's fine!"

The tides tell tales of laughter and cheer,
"We're not just waves, we're friends here, dear!"
With an ebb and flow, they dance so bold,
While shells giggle at stories retold.

Through the salty air, our spirits climb,
Floating along with the rhythms of time.
Tides may crash and moments may flee,
But laughter's the treasure we carry to sea!

Secrets of the Ancients

Once upon a time, they said,
Old trees gossip while we're in bed.
With whispers from the past they share,
Filling dreams with tales of hair.

A raccoon once wore a crown of leaves,
Claimed wisdom just might come from thieves.
The squirrels chuckled, 'He's lost his nut!'
The wise old oak just said, 'Good luck!'

Mossy volumes, dusty and neat,
Fell open to reveal their feat.
In ancient scrolls, we find a joke,
To laugh so hard, we nearly choke.

So gather round, let's heed the cue,
For ages past have much to do.
With laughter echoing through the woods,
Ancients smile, "Hey, life's pretty good!"

Buried Truths

Digging deep beneath the ground,
A treasure trove of truth is found.
But who would think, amid the dirt,
That buried truths wear lots of hurt?

A gnome once hid a sock and shoe,
Swore they contained a secret or two.
But when we found them, what a sight!
Just a ghost's laundry, nothing bright.

The old bones chuckled, "Let's just laugh,
Life's more fun on the silly path."
So when you dig for wisdom's gold,
You might just find some stories old.

Some truths might smell of sweet decay,
With roses blooming on the way.
The lesson's clear—don't take it all,
For buried truths can make us fall!

The Fabric of Being

Threads entwined in colors bright,
Stitching life with sheer delight.
Yet one loose thread begins to rhyme,
A sock sings songs of silly time.

Tangled tales of joy and dread,
Fabric hides what's left unsaid.
A button bids the old to stay,
While pockets hoard the dreams of play.

Warp and weft in motion spin,
We weave our laughter deep within.
A patchwork quilt of quirks and dreams,
Unraveled stitches, bursting seams.

So when you seam the fabric's grace,
Remember folly's woven face.
For woven laughter can outweigh,
The heavy threads of everyday.

Ties that Bind

Knots of friendship, strong and strange,
Brought us laughter, made us change.
A bow on top, or a big old tie,
Can lift our spirits, let us fly.

A cat and dog share a big embrace,
Tangled up in a silly chase.
They trip on leashes, fall with flair,
While neighbors stop to gawk and stare.

What binds us all? A shared delight,
In tangled webs, we find our flight.
So grab a friend and spin around,
In laughter's bond, true joy is found.

For ties that bind can also break,
But let's be real—let's make mistakes!
The jumbled moments, laughter's hue,
Are ties that bind and see us through!

A Tapestry of Heritage

In grandma's garden, weeds parade,
Beneath the flowers, secrets laid.
Uncle Joe's stories, tall as trees,
Tickle my ribs with quirky tease.

Aunt Mabel paints with colors bright,
Every shade an epic sight.
Each stitch in time a hearty laugh,
As family ties get wrapped in craft.

Cousins play hopscotch on the sod,
Arguing over who's the fraud.
But when the pie comes into view,
All feuds dissolve; we all want two.

Through quilted patches, chuckles soar,
In every fold, there's room for more.
Heritage ties, like silly strings,
Make merry chaos out of things.

The Hidden Ties

Behind the laughter, whispers play,
A cousin's crush, we won't convey.
In grandma's hat, a rabbit hides,
Join us for a wild ride.

When long-lost relatives appear,
We pretend we have no fear.
The family tree's a twisted vine,
With roots so deep, they intertwine.

Aunt Sue makes jokes with a straight face,
While Uncle Bob's lost in his own race.
Shared desserts are the sweetest ties,
As everyone winks with shifty eyes.

In photo albums, truth's disguised,
With every snapshot, giggles rise.
Hidden ties in each little frame,
Life's intricate and fun, not the same.

Roots in Stillness

In the quiet of the yard, they sprout,
All the stories we joke about.
Dad's old recliner, a kingdom vast,
Where royal decrees are made at last.

Under the surface, treasures dwell,
Like Aunt June's secrets, we all know well.
Every branch a ticklish giggle,
In stillness, family ties do wiggle.

A game of charades by the tree,
Acting out a gopher, or maybe a bee.
Our laughter mingles with the breeze,
While roots dig in and everyone sees.

Old photos hide behind the door,
Where memories dance and spill on the floor.
In stillness, the echoes loudly sing,
A symphony of what we all bring.

Interwoven Stories

In the tapestry of quirky tales,
Every thread a laugh that never pales.
Aunt Clara's cat in a silly hat,
Brought giggles to every chat.

Uncle Fred dances like a pro,
On a pogo stick, putting on a show.
While stories weave in double knots,
The punchlines land, tying up lots.

Dinner table debates, wild and loud,
Where every theory makes us proud.
A sergeant major in a funny suit,
Marching to the beat of a hoot.

In the fabric of our funny plight,
Interwoven stories shine so bright.
With hooks and laughter all around,
In family bonds, joy is found.

Wildflowers of Thought

In the garden of my mind, they bloom,
Thoughts dance like daisies, dispelling gloom.
A poppy whispers jokes from afar,
While tulips giggle under the star.

I once had a dream to climb a tree,
But forgot that I'm not as spry as I be.
So I sit with my weeds, feeling quite grand,
And pass the time making up a band.

Sunflowers nodding with silly grins,
Laughing at all of my foolish sins.
A daffodil winks, it's no sin to play,
As I weave wild tales from night until day.

So here's to my thoughts, both wild and free,
Sprouting in laughter, come join me, wee.
In this garden of jests, I'll plant my cheer,
And nurture the smiles all throughout the year.

The Quiet Embrace

In a world of whispers, secrets unfurl,
A squirrel drops acorns, plans to pearl.
The breeze is a messenger, giggling in jest,
Hiding in shadows, it's quite the guest.

Quiet moments dance on the tip of a twig,
Where thoughts tip-toe, and feelings dig.
A tree stretches wide, embracing the sun,
While ants hold conferences, plotting for fun.

The pond chuckles softly, rippling with mirth,
Reflecting the clouds as they dance, giving birth.
A frog croaks a tune, it's quite a sight,
While fireflies boogie, lighting up the night.

So let's cherish whispers that quietly sing,
In the gentle embrace of every small thing.
Laugh with the breeze, let the quiet proclaim,
The joy found in stillness, a whimsical game.

Horizons of Yesterday

Yesterday's clouds were a sight to behold,
Like cotton candy dreams, both fluffy and bold.
I chased them around, hoping to catch,
A flavor of laughter, a sunbeam to snatch.

Time hops like a rabbit, quite eager to play,
Bouncing through moments that fade away.
I reminisce on the flops, giggles they bring,
As the past winks at me, oh what a fling!

Old socks on the line wave like flags of cheer,
Reminding me how life twists with no fear.
Like a kite in the breeze, I soar and I dive,
Piecing together all the moments I thrive.

So toast to the yesterdays, wild and untamed,
Each laugh a horizon, never quite named.
With the sun dipping down, painting the skies,
I wave back at memories, wearing their ties.

Meditations in the Meadow

In the meadow, I ponder, with daisies as guides,
Where thoughts bounce like bunnies, in humorous strides.

Butterflies flutter, adding whimsy to air,
I sit with my musings, without a care.

Each blade of grass has a story to tell,
Of ticklish winds that ring a lovely bell.
A ladybug chuckles, struts on my shoe,
As the daisies gossip of skies colored blue.

Crickets compose symphonies under the stars,
While fireflies flicker like miniature cars.
I find in their dance, a silly delight,
A meditation that twirls in the soft light.

So here in the meadow, laughter takes root,
As I gather my dreams like a big, quirky fruit.
In this playful expanse where whimsies collide,
I cherish the moments, my heart opened wide.

Beneath the Canopy

Under leafy greens we hang,
Sipping tea while squirrels clang.
Laughter floats like dandelion seeds,
Nature's jokes fulfill our needs.

Birds overhead sing off-key,
Tapping feet of the buzzing bee.
A raccoon steals my sandwich slice,
While I ponder if that's nice.

The sun peeks through with a cheeky grin,
A gentle breeze tries to sneak in.
Why did the tree go to the party?
It had to branch out—how hearty!

So we sit and giggle away,
While shadows dance and children play.
In the forest, where humor grows,
Plant a smile and watch it glow.

Everlasting Ties

Dancing roots beneath the ground,
Whisper secrets without a sound.
Old tree stumps give the best advice,
'Get out more, it's worth the price!'

A worm winks; he's had his fun,
Traveling far when day is done.
'Why chase leaves?' he says with glee,
'When all I need is here with me!'

Branches sway like they've got moves,
Strutting grooves that nature proves.
When limbs get tired, take a break,
Nap in sunshine, make no mistake!

Roots entwined in a funny dance,
Nature's jesters, given a chance.
Through thick and thin, we stay aligned,
Our friendships, forever twined.

The Weight of Stillness

In a world that likes to rush,
Sitting still feels quite a hush.
Chuckling leaves, they know the game,
As branches bow, they take the blame.

A wise old log holds court with ants,
'They call me slow, but I take my chance!'
While time drips slow like honey's flow,
Patience here is the way to go.

Objects in motion, time to catch,
A leaf falls down, what a perfect match!
Quirky time, with a twist and turn,
Moments freeze, where giggles churn.

So let's embrace that quiet beat,
Finding fun in every seat.
For stillness holds a hidden jest,
A playful heart knows where it's best.

Silent Roots of Wisdom

Beneath the soil, wisdom sleeps,
Telling tales that nature keeps.
Though silent, roots whisper wise,
'Look up, my friend, to the clear blue skies!'

Sometimes they chuckle at passing feet,
'Hey, where you going? You can't compete!'
Little explorers, they stop and stare,
'Adventure awaits, if you dare!'

Old knots and gnarls, like an old man's face,
Hold stories of eons, a timeless grace.
But don't be fooled by the solemn ways,
They've seen the funny sides of days!

So next time you wander in a grove,
Remember the laughter that old trees wove.
In nature's stay, take a little pause—
For wisdom chuckles without a cause.

Veils of Green

In the garden, plants wear hats,
A cactus juggling with the bats,
Leaves gossip while sipping dew,
And flowers dance, oh what a view!

A snail races an old toad's leap,
While daisies giggle, their secrets keep,
The soil whispers tales to spry,
As sunlight winks up in the sky!

Mice hold meetings by the fence,
Debating cheese, it's all so tense,
But watch the hedgehog roll on by,
With hedges like a fluffy tie!

Vines twirl around a wooden post,
Grinning at the sun, they boast,
In this haven where laughter's spry,
Nature chuckles, oh my my!

Solitude Under the Stars

A lone frog croaks beneath the moon,
While crickets share a secret tune,
Stars wink down, a bright parade,
While owls joke in the leafy shade.

The night air's thick with playful dreams,
As shadows dance in silver beams,
An acorn dreams of being grand,
As squirrels laugh at their own plans.

Fireflies put on a light show,
While soft winds swish to and fro,
The night is full of giggles bright,
As sleepy critters bid goodnight.

In solitude, they share a laugh,
As nature paints a joyful path,
With voices soft, they sway and prance,
Creating joy in their wild dance!

Memories in the Soil

Down below where critters play,
The roots hold stories of the day,
Worms recall the rain's delight,
While beetles cheer, 'What a night!'

The mushrooms claim the latest scoop,
Of garden parties in a group,
Each dirt clump holds a memory,
Like a wooden chair, oh so comfy!

In cuddly corners, herbs exchange,
Their best-kept jokes, a little strange,
A thyme plant slips a pun or two,
While sage just laughs and adds some hue.

Roots giggle in a tangled ball,
Each tiny strand a funny call,
Their whispers swirl in earthy tones,
Planting joy among the stones!

Growth through Trials

A sprout pushes through the ground so tough,
While weeds shout, 'You're not enough!'
But with a grin, the buds reply,
'We rise with laughter, watch us fly!'

The raindrops tease, so bold and spry,
While storms howl, 'You think you'll cry?'
But every drop fuels up their cheer,
Each challenge met with a hearty jeer!

Roots tangle up in playful fights,
While nature spins its dizzy nights,
Through every twist, they find their way,
And giggles bloom beneath the fray!

With every bruise, they grow so wise,
In sunshine days or cloudy skies,
Embracing life, come what may,
These plants know it's all a game to play!

The Network of Time

In tangled webs of days gone by,
We stumble like a baby fly.
Remembering when socks were lost,
And laughter blooms at every cost.

Each tick of clocks a friendly jest,
A dance of years we can't contest.
Like squirrels in a frantic race,
Chasing memories we can't replace.

With each misstep, we chuckle loud,
Reflecting on our former crowd.
Time's a trickster, yes indeed,
Playing games while we all heed.

So raise a glass to days of yore,
With funny tales of life's uproar.
In this great network, we entwine,
A tapestry of laughs, divine.

Whispering Groves of Memory

In groves where whispers softly play,
Old stories bloom like flowers in May.
Tales of mishaps, oh so grand,
Like dancing bears on shifting sand.

Each tree holds secrets, roots so deep,
Of silly dreams that make us leap.
I tripped on thoughts, and how they flew,
In echoing laughter, we found our crew.

The sunbeams giggle, teasing light,
As shadows join the playful fight.
With every breeze, a chuckle shared,
In this enchanted place, we've dared.

So let the laughter fill the air,
With memories that dance and flare.
In whispering groves, we take our stand,
United in joy, a silly band.

Enshrined in Earth

Beneath the soil, where secrets sleep,
Are tales of clumsiness that deeply creep.
Like worms that wiggle out of sight,
They dance with glee in morning light.

In every root, a giggle found,
As plants discuss the antics round.
"Remember when we missed the rain?"
Now earth's a stage, and roots entertain!

Up springs a flower, all aglow,
"You think you're clever, but low you go!"
And while they chat, we sit and muse,
On earthy tales we couldn't refuse.

So let us toast to dirt and roots,
To memories clad in leafy suits.
In the earth's embrace, laughter swirls,
An ode to life, to silly whirls.

Fulcrum of the Past

At the pivot where time does swirl,
We find our place, oh what a whirl!
With laughter echoing through the trees,
We giggle and tumble like autumn leaves.

Here stands the fulcrum, strong yet spry,
Balancing moments, oh me, oh my!
A bumpy ride on history's street,
With stumbles that lead to tales quite sweet.

With every joke, a memory thrives,
Like jester hats on long-lost drives.
We raise a smile, a chuckle bright,
At the fulcrum where wrong feels right.

In this carnival of yore we play,
Making light of each clumsy sway.
So here's to times both wacky and fast,
In this amusement park of the past.

Twisted Tendrils of Truth

In a garden where weeds like to tease,
I found a gnome hiding behind the trees.
He grinned and he chuckled, what a sight to behold,
Said, 'Life's a bit twisted, but never too old!'

With roots that entwine like a silly old dance,
The daisies and dandelions join in the prance.
They laugh at the sun and tickle the ground,
Claiming their space as the funnest around!

The carrots debate with the pesky young flies,
While petunias puff up, acting oh-so-wise.
"I'm pretty, I'm witty, a sight for sore eyes!"
The lettuce just sulks, wishing for fries.

But amidst all the humor, a lesson rings clear,
Life's a wild joke; let's celebrate here!
So let the gnome giggle, let flowers take turns,
In the garden of laughter, for joy is what burns!

Seeds of Contemplation

In a pot by the window, a seed sat and thought,
'There's more to this life than what's readily sought.'
A pebble nearby, muttering with flair,
'Just wait till it rains; I'll show you I care!'

The sun peeks in, shining light on their chat,
The seed stretches out, 'I wish I was that!'
But the pebble just chuckles and gives a sly grin,
'Sunburns, my friend, are where fun begins!'

As clouds roll in, they play hide and seek,
The seed learns that patience isn't for the weak.
"Don't rush the good stuff; let nature take charge!"
Said the pebble, who knew how to live large.

So cheers to the seeds that ponder and stew,
In a world full of wonder, adventures ensue.
Each ponderous thought like a sprout growing high,
Laughing at life while reaching for the sky!

Echoing Memoria

In a forest so dense, where echoes abound,
Sat a tree with a story, and the funniest sound.
It told tales of squirrels and their acorn heists,
Of hiccupping owls and moonlit feasts, what a feast!

Each branch held a memory, swaying in jest,
Like whispers of laughter that nature knows best.
A breeze carried secrets through leaves up to the sky,
'Is this the punchline?' they asked, oh my, oh my!

The mushrooms chuckled, with caps all aglow,
'We're the comedians; we steal the show!'
With every soft giggle, the forest would sway,
Turning seriousness into a playful ballet.

From shadows to sunlight, the echoes took flight,
With laughter resounding, both day and night.
So let's dance with the trees, and let stories unfold,
For in laughter and memories, true magic is told!

Boughs of Perspective

Under boughs that twist like a funny old grin,
A monkey swung by with a mischievous spin.
He shouted, 'Hey everyone, gather around,
Life's a blend of nuts and silliness found!'

The turtles were slow, but they joined in the jest,
'With all this good humor, we feel pretty blessed!'
The rabbits chimed in, with a hop and a wiggle,
'Laugh hard and long! We'll dance a big jiggle!'

Each bough held a view, quirky and neat,
The daisies debated who has the best seat.
While grasshoppers chirped from high top their reeds,
'We're the chorus of laughter while nature feeds!'

As sunbeams cascaded and shadows played tricks,
Life's moments stacked up like good old party bricks.
So swing with the monkeys and twirl in delight,
In this jungle of laughter, everything feels right!

The Essence of Earth

Beneath the dirt, I found my shoe,
A garden gnome, just passing through.
I asked him why he looked so glum,
He said, 'I lost my head. Well, ain't that dumb!'

Worms talk gossip, oh so loud,
While flowers dance, feeling proud.
A tree once whispered sweetly to me,
But all I caught was, 'Bark like a bee!'

Mushrooms giggled, spread their cheer,
As ants marched by, with snacks to share.
A frog croaked jokes, ribbiting fast,
I laughed so hard, fell flat on grass!

The essence swirls in playful jest,
Nature's jokes, she loves the best.
So next time you stroll under the sun,
Remember, giggles with roots are fun!

Below the Horizon

The clouds were wearing pajamas, so sweet,
As I searched for my lost left shoe on the street.
The sun popped up, a bright, round clown,
Throwing confetti while upside down.

Rabbits with shades, hopping with flair,
Danced on the rooftops like they just didn't care.
A squirrel was breakdancing, feeling quite fine,
The branches swayed in a groove, so divine.

Below the horizon, the silliness grows,
With daisies and dandelions, striking a pose.
I found my shoe, it was tied to a kite,
Caught up in laughter, oh, what a sight!

So let your heart frolic where skies are blue,
Join nature's circus, it's waiting for you!
Below the horizon, the fun won't cease,
With a chuckle and grin, let laughter increase!

Intertwined Memories

In the garden of giggles, my mind's in a twist,
I thought of a snail who couldn't resist.
He said, 'I'm late for my shell's big parade!'
I laughed so hard, I almost swayed!

Tangled up vines, with secrets to share,
A rabbit's wise words floated in the air.
'Never chew grass when a hawk's on the prowl,'
Echoes of chuckles from a nearby owl.

The memories dance, twirling in glee,
A dance partnership with an old cherry tree.
Every leaf has a story, a rumor, a pun,
In this wacky wonderland, we're all just having fun!

So gather your laughter, plant it deep,
In the soil of joy, where the quirks never sleep.
Intertwined in the absurd, hold tight the thread,
For the garden of memories is where dreams are bred!

Where Shadows Meet Light

A shadow looked in the mirror today,
And said, 'Why do I always fade away?'
With a wink, the sunshine replied in delight,
'You're just hiding, come out of the night!'

Laughter echoed through the leafy glades,
As the sun played tag with the playful shades.
A raccoon pranced, with a mask so slick,
"Hide and seek is better with a light-hearted trick!"

Where shadows meet light, giggles abound,
In puddles of joy where silliness is found.
The flowers chuckle, their petals all blushed,
With bees buzzing softly, their rhythm all hushed.

So dance with your shadows, let laughter ignite,
Where joy steals the show, and the world feels right.
For even in darkness, a chuckle takes flight,
Bringing smiles to the day, where shadows meet light!

The Wisdom of the Ages

Old trees tell tales, their branches sway,
Squirrels taking bets on who'll fall today.
Leaves gossip secrets, in wind's delight,
Nature's comedians, they own the night.

Moss soft as pillows, beds for the shy,
Frogs sing operas, croaking on high.
Raccoons in tuxedos, dignified sass,
Dancing beneath stars, they're first in class.

Roots whisper gossip, oh what a twist,
Tangled connections, no chance to resist.
Trees in the backseat, just trying to steer,
Laughing at humans, who drink too much beer.

A wise old oak gives advice to a sprout,
"Grow a thick bark, it's what life's about!"
But little ones giggle at old folks' fears,
"Just bend with the wind; it'll reduce your tears!"

Bark and Breath

Bark's got jokes, it chuckles at night,
While leaves high-five with the passing light.
Twisting roots play hopscotch below,
As branches laugh quietly, putting on a show.

Sap drips like secrets, sticky and bold,
Stories from trees, just waiting to be told.
Air full of whispers, like giggling sprites,
Mirth in the shadows, what a great sight!

Fungi wear hats, dressed up to impress,
Mushrooms discussing their flowery dress.
Worms in their burrows plot parties and feasts,
Squirrels bring snacks, nature's wild beasts.

In this green theater where laughter is free,
Life's just a comedy, come sit with me.
Watch the trees dancing, their roots in a tangle,
Joy in the forest, we all must wrangle.

Nurtured by Silence

In the calm of the woods, still moments arise,
Trees hold their breath, taking in the skies.
Raccoons play charades under moon's soft light,
The woods hold their laughter till morning's first bite.

A chipmunk with swagger, takes his grand stand,
Claiming the acorn, "It's all mine, understand?"
Whispers of breezes, tickle the trunk,
Nature's own stage, where the critters debunk.

Laughter erupts, like bubbles in soup,
As beetles join in on the willowy troop.
Moss says, "Shh, let the quiet take charge,"
But even the silence is vibrant and large.

The forest thus cradles its soft, gentle glee,
In shadows so deep, funny antics we see.
A nutty ensemble, the wild roots ahead,
Echoes of laughter while resting our head.

Tranquil Depths

Under the surface, the chatter's a blast,
Fish swap tall tales, their friendships are vast.
Shadows of plants do the tango in streams,
Life's just a party, all woven in dreams.

Bubbles like giggles rise up to the sky,
Life swims along, with a wink and a sigh.
Crabs in their shells wear hats all askew,
Making sure everyone sees their fine view.

In pools of reflection, the frogs draw their lines,
Debating the best way to catch the spring pines.
"Do I hop or do I swim?" one rants in despair,
While tadpoles just chuckle, "We haven't a care!"

Joy blooms like lilies, bright colors and cheer,
Every ripple dances, nothing to fear.
Laughing it off, what a splendid affair,
Nature's own laughter, around everywhere.

Veins of Existence

Underneath the ground so deep,
Worms have secrets they can't keep.
Sipping joy from muddy streams,
They laugh at our wildest dreams.

Roots do yoga, stretch and sway,
In their home where squirrels play.
Digging holes with little paws,
They're the garden's laughing laws.

Sunbeams tickle every sprout,
While shadows dance and twist about.
A leaf's a hat, a flower's a smile,
Nature's jesters, in perfect style.

With every gust, they shake and twirl,
With whispers of the earth, they whirl.
In this realm of glee and grime,
Life's a joke, a funny rhyme.

Subterranean Stories

Down below where moles reside,
They spin tall tales with worms as guide.
Rabbits gossip about the tree,
Fashion tips from ants, oh my, you see!

The roots conspire, a gossip crew,
Planning pranks, oh what a view!
Roses wear thorns like crowns,
While daisies giggle in their gowns.

Each sugar ant, a tiny thief,
Stealing crumbs, spreading belief.
They tell of feasts and wild delight,
In the soil's warm, cozy night.

Funny echoes bounce around,
Stories shared without a sound.
We laugh, we tumble, with great surprise,
In this crazy underground paradise.

Nourished by Time

Time's a chef with a leafy plate,
Cooking up laughs, oh, how they wait.
Zucchini sprouts with a side of peas,
Joking 'bout life in the swaying breeze.

Bees buzz softly, sharing their buzz,
Telling the trees, 'It's all just a fuzz!'
Carrots nodding in their orange cheer,
Saying, 'Don't worry, we're all still here!'

The pumpkins chuckle, split at the seam,
'Growing wise is just a big dream!'
They all root for the sun each day,
A round of giggles, hooray, hooray!

As time tiptoes, the shadows dance,
Every petal has a second chance.
With laughter woven through the soil,
Our fun-filled hearts, we gently spoil.

Hidden Currents

Rivers whisper beneath my feet,
Cracking jokes about the heat.
Fish joke about a worm parade,
As turtles take a sheltered shade.

Winds carry tales from tree to tree,
'Can you believe that leaf's a she?'
Down by the brook, frogs break into song,
'Join us now, it won't take long!'

Streams prance over pebbles with glee,
Bubbling laughter, wild and free.
Oh, the stones hear every pun,
While giggling crickets join in the fun.

In this dance of joyous sound,
Nature's humor can astound.
With hidden currents, laughter flows,
In the roots below, where laughter grows.

Silent Murmurs of Legacy

In a garden of whispers, I tread,
Where gnomes hold secrets, long since said.
They chuckle and wink, oh what a show,
As I trip on my roots, move fast or slow.

Old oak trees gossip as winds gently tease,
About squirrels who think they're the kings of the trees.
I'd join their fun, but I'm stuck in this spot,
Laughing so hard, I forgot what I thought.

Grandpa's old shovel still rests in the shade,
Thinking of digging a grand escapade.
But the weeds grew thicker, much to my dread,
With each passing day, they raised more instead.

So here I am, lost in the play,
Hearing leaves giggle and dance all day.
I'll keep my ears open, my roots tight and true,
For I'm part of this show, just like all of you.

A Tapestry of Time

Weaving through moments, I trip and I fall,
Like a spider in spandex, I'm stuck on the wall.
Each thread a memory, bright like a bloom,
I laugh at the chaos, my life's crazy room.

A needle, a button, and quite a few seams,
My quilt's like a saga, stitched from my dreams.
The patches a riot, a carnival bright,
Each snip a reminder of joy and of fright.

Stitching old stories, I twist and I turn,
Dodging the fabric of lessons I learn.
Some colors are vibrant, others a mess,
But each holds a tale, I think I'm so blessed.

In this quilt of my life, there's laughter and tears,
Ironing out wrinkles from all of my years.
Though threads may unravel, I'll laugh with delight,
For it's all part of living, a colorful fight.

The Depths of Contemplation

In the pond of my thoughts, I see a frog,
Jumping through ripples, oh what a slog!
He thinks he's a prince, but oh what a show,
The flies hover close—what a feast they'll throw!

Pondering deeply, I stare at the sky,
As fish flash their secrets, swimming right by.
The bubbles raise questions, then burst with a pop,
Wondering if this is where wisdom will stop.

A turtle nearby, so wise and so slow,
Tells me to chill, just let it all flow.
But my thoughts are a whirlwind, spinning in glee,
They bounce like a beach ball, just wait and you'll see!

So I swim in my musings, the waves rise and fall,
Wishing the turtles would lighten their call.
For here in this pond, while pondering fate,
I'm just a bit goofy, and honestly late.

Embracing the Unseen

In a fog of confusion, I dance with my shoes,
Not knowing at all if it's really the blues.
A shadow passed by, I giggled a cheer,
Was it a ghost, or just my lost beer?

I whisper to secrets hidden in air,
They chuckle and vanish, oh where could they fare?
Every unseen corner can spin quite a tale,
You'd laugh at the thoughts that dance on my veil.

The echoes of laughter bounce back from the walls,
As I chase phantoms in bright purple halls.
With playful persistence, I leap and I glide,
Making friends with the things no one else tried.

So here I am, in a world that can't see,
Bringing forth joy from what normally be.
With giggles and tickles, I run with the breeze,
For life's just a game, come play if you please!

Embracing Earth's Memories

Dancing in the soil, I found my shoe,
The worms had a party, they joined in too.
With giggles and wiggles, they swayed all night,
As roots gave a cheer, what a silly sight!

Socks in the garden, what a strange place,
Befriended a squirrel, oh what a face!
He told me his secrets, but I lost the thread,
Now I'm just wondering how to bribe a hedgehog instead.

Underneath the Surface

Digging through dirt, what's that? A fork?
The garden gnome chuckled, said it's my cork.
Time travel through lettuce, I'm tasting the past,
But carrots sing ballads, and the peas are fast.

Potatoes can whisper, I swear they have plans,
While radishes giggle, and tell terrible puns.
I thought I was wise, but they had a ball,
Now I'm a jester, in a vegetable hall.

Echoes of the Ancients

Old tree by the path, what tales do you spin?
You've seen all the folks who forgot their bin.
With a sigh he recalled, the days of old,
When trees wore hats, made of vibrant gold.

Squirrels, the ninjas, in stealthy formation,
Stealing my snacks, what's their motivation?
Roots intertwined, a secret pact made,
To laugh at the human, and their picnic parade.

Nourished by Time

In the soil we find, tales full of cheer,
Of onions with giggles and peppers with beer.
The sun shines bright; it's a party for sure,
With nature's own DJ, and a bass made of bur.

Time slips away, like a worm on a run,
What did I plant? Oh boy, this is fun!
Zucchini in tutus, they dance with a flair,
While broccoli bows, with a top hat to wear.

Anchored in Essence

In a garden where veggies wear hats,
A tomato declared, 'I'm too round for chats!'
With carrots in shades, they danced with glee,
Saying, 'Let's all root for a tea party!'

All the daisies gossip in petals of pink,
While the radishes ponder, avoiding the sink.
The beans made a band, with their rhythm so fine,
But no one would dance, for they lost track of time.

The Heart of the Landscape

The sunflowers twirled in a pirouette,
While soil beneath giggled, a messy vignette.
A mushroom declared, 'I'm a fancy hotel!'
But guests always left with a 'toadstool' smell.

The wind chuckled softly, whispering jokes,
As the bushes cracked up at the antics of folks.
And once in a while, a butterfly pranced,
While the weeds in the corner were just caught entranced.

Sunkissed Introspection

In the shade of a tree, a wise worm laid low,
Said, 'Life is a fruit salad, don't you know?'
The apples all laughed, 'We're the stars of the show!'
While the lettuce just sighed, 'I'd rather not grow.'

A lizard with sunglasses sunned on a rock,
Claimed he'd start yoga, to look like a clock.
The pond frogs would croak, 'Try it, why wait?'
But the lizard just snoozed; it's all about fate.

Cultivating Inner Landscapes

A cactus once dreamed of a lush tropical isle,
With pineapples laughing in their prickly style.
The succulents whispered, 'A beach vacation?'
But sand got stuck where they needed elation!

The mint leaves squabbled over whose drink was best,
While the thyme said, 'Guys, I'm just here for the zest!'
The flowers designed a 'Sip and Giggle' night,
But bees stole the spotlight, buzzing with delight.

The Ties That Bind

In a garden where gossip grows,
Upside-down carrots wear big bows.
Beans spill secrets to potatoes,
While peas roll laughter in rows.

A flower's shade holds tales unspoken,
While daisies dance, their heads unbroken.
The sun's a friend, with jokes to lend,
As roots shake hands, a gaggle woken.

Worms whisper sweet nothings below,
As bees get busy, stealing the show.
Every sprout knows when it's time to laugh,
In this patch, it's a comic tableau.

So dig your laughter, plant it deep,
In every corner, sow the giggle heap.
For in this patch of green delight,
Together we bloom, and silliness leaps.

Veins of History

Underneath the tangled vines,
Old leaves hold tales of former times.
A gnarled root grins, wisdom shared,
While beetles roll like little mimes.

Tales of trees that wore a crown,
And nuts that fell, with little frown.
A squirrel's jest becomes a lore,
As branches sway, up and down.

Rabbits gossip with a bent twig,
While fog plays tag, it's all a gig.
Each season turns, a comedy show,
In the arboreal dance, life's big jig.

So join the fun, take a peek,
At nature's scrapbook, full and sleek.
History's vein is filled with cheer,
In every laugh, there's joy we seek.

Speaking with the Soil

The earth below has tales to tell,
Of mischief made in a mossy dell.
Worms are the gossiping old fools,
While roots share tea, beneath the shell.

They chuckle at stones, lying still,
With dirt's own chatter, ha! What a thrill!
Every pebble's a rumor spread,
As worms write notes with a bent quill.

A dandelion's giggles rise,
As radishes wear comedic guise.
The soil's a stage for every jest,
In this earthy play, laughter flies.

So next time you plant, take a seat,
And listen close, the humor's sweet.
For in every patch that's planted right,
The soil spills laughter, quite the treat.

Beneath the Canopy

Under the leaves, in a shady nook,
Where acorns fall, and squirrels cook.
Each critter shares a funny flare,
While branches sway, and laughter's hooked.

A crow cracks jokes while perched on high,
As chipmunks giggle, oh my, oh my!
The sun, a spotlight, bursts through green,
As shadows dance, their spirits fly.

It's a comedy club, painted with bark,
Where every rustle ignites a spark.
From roots to canopies, they conspire,
To drag in the light, a vibrant arc.

So take a stroll, join the jest,
In nature's laugh, you'll find the best.
For beneath the green, hilarity blooms,
An endless giggle, a joyous rest.

www.ingramcontent.com/pod-product-compliance
Lightning Source LLC
Chambersburg PA
CBHW071824160426
43209CB00003B/201